anything

D0548715

Redbeard

Cavendish Square
New York

Rebecca Stefoff

Published in 2015 by Cavendish Square Publishing, LLC
243 5th Avenue, Suite 136, New York, NY 10016

First Edition

Website: cavendishsq.com

CPSIA Compliance Information: Batch #WW15CSQ

All websites were available and accurate when this book was sent to press.

Library of Congress Cataloging-in-Publication Data

Stefoff, Rebecca, 1951-
Redbeard / Rebecca Stefoff.
pages cm. — (True-life pirates)
Includes bibliographical references and index.
ISBN 978-1-50260-199-5 (hardcover) ISBN 978-1-50260-198-8 (ebook)
1. Barbarossa, -1546—Juvenile literature. 2. Admirals—Turkey—Biography—Juvenile literature. 3. Pirates—Turkey—Biography—Juvenile literature. 4. Pirates—Africa, North—Biography—Juvenile literature. 5. Pirates—Mediterranean Region—History—16th century—Juvenile literature. I. Title.

DR509.B22S74 2015
910.4'5—dc23

2014024980

Editorial Director: David McNamara
Editor: Andrew Coddington
Copy Editor: Cynthia Roby
Art Director: Jeffrey Talbot

Senior Designer: Amy Greenan
Senior Production Manager: Jennifer Ryder-Talbot
Production Editor: Sam Cochrane
Photo Research: J8 Media

Printed in the United States of America

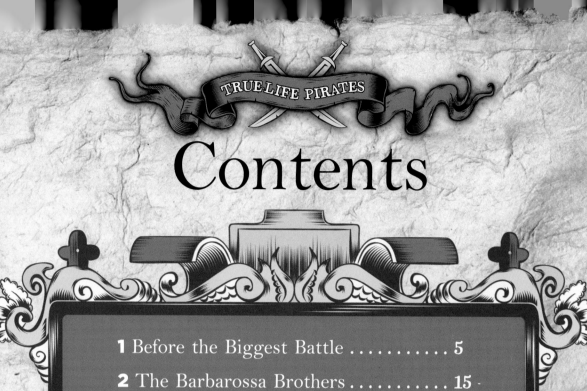

Contents

one

Before the Biggest Battle

On a September day in 1538, an argument raged aboard the flagship of the Turkish navy, anchored off the town of Preveza on the western coast of Greece. The ship was the headquarters of the high **admiral** of the navy, a man feared and respected in all the lands around the Mediterranean Sea. He was known as Kheir-ed-Din Barbarossa, or Redbeard. He had been chosen by the **sultan**, the supreme ruler of the Turks, to command the Turkish navy in a massive battle.

Barbarossa, or Redbeard, appears noble and fearless in this scene of a battle at sea.

The emperor Suleiman the Magnificent turned a pirate into an admiral.

The Turkish navy was preparing to clash with a navy made up of forces from many of the nations of Europe. Pope Paul III, the head of the Christian faith in Europe, had called together the huge fleet and ordered it to wipe out the forces of the Muslim Turks, and to stop their commander, Barbarossa, from attacking Christian towns. Even before the two fleets met, however, Barbarossa faced trouble from his own senior officers.

Many of those officers came from noble families. They had spent their lives in the Turkish army or navy and did not think that they should take orders from Barbarossa, who was a commoner. Barbarossa had come from a humble background. Just a few years earlier he had been a **corsair**, as pirates based in the Mediterranean were called.

High-ranking army officers who had sailed with the Turkish fleet wanted to land soldiers on the coast to keep the enemy from landing there. Barbarossa argued that men on shore would be easy targets for the mighty cannons of the European ships. After much argument, though, Barbarossa gave in. He allowed Murad **Reis**, one of the most eager officers, to lead a force of armed men onto the beach. Just as Barbarossa had warned, Murad's men were cut down in great numbers by cannon fire from the Europeans, whose guns were bigger and more powerful than those of the Turks. Murad and his surviving soldiers retreated, leaving many of their comrades dead on the sand. Barbarossa had been right. Landing the troops was a deadly mistake.

From that moment forward, Barbarossa's word was law in his fleet. Barbarossa was determined that the great battle would be fought at sea, not by soldiers going ashore to clash on land. The only question was whether the Turkish navy could defeat the larger and more powerfully armed European fleet.

The Battle of Preveza would be the most important battle of Barbarossa's long and violent career. It would also settle the fate of the Mediterranean for decades to come.

The Rise of the Ottoman Empire

The Battle of Preveza was part of a centuries-long war between the Christian powers of Europe and the **Ottoman Empire**, a Muslim state based in Turkey. Before the Ottoman Empire began, however, two major events set the course of history around the Mediterranean. One event was the splitting of the old Roman Empire. The other was the rise of Islam in Arabia.

In 395 AD the Roman Empire was divided into two parts. The Western Empire was based in Italy, birthplace of the Roman civilization. The Eastern

Empire was based in the city of Constantinople, in what is now Turkey. When the Western Empire collapsed from barbarian invasions, the Eastern Empire became known as the Byzantine Empire. Both empires were Christian, although they followed different versions of Christianity.

A few hundred years later, in the seventh century AD, the religion of Islam was born in the Arabian Peninsula. The Arabs who adopted this new faith were known as Muslims. They quickly spread Islam and the Arabic language to neighboring regions, including Egypt, North Africa, and parts of the Middle East and Central Asia. The central and eastern parts of Turkey became Islamic, under the control of many chieftains, or **emirs**. The western edge of Turkey remained under the control of the Byzantine Empire, along with much of Greece and the lands in the Balkan Mountains of southeastern Europe.

In 1299, the emir of one of the Muslim Turkish states, a man named Osman, declared himself sultan, or ruler over the other states. He conquered some of them. Others joined him voluntarily. This was the beginning of the Ottoman Empire.

For a century and a half the rising power of the Ottomans chipped away at the Byzantine Empire. The Turks conquered cities and whole regions, including parts of Greece and Bulgaria. Finally, in 1453, they conquered Constantinople itself, and the Byzantine Empire came to an end. The Byzantine city of Constantinople—known today as Istanbul—became the new Ottoman capital. In 1538, when Barbarossa was getting ready to fight the Battle of Preveza, the sultan of the Ottoman

Ships with both oars and sails were used in the Mediterranean for war, trade—and piracy.

Empire was Suleiman the Magnificent. It was during his reign that Ottoman power reached its height.

Warfare on the Waves

Pirates, merchants, and navies of Barbarossa's time sailed the Mediterranean in **galleys**, a kind of ship that had been used since ancient times. A galley was powered by rowers. Stationed all along both sides of the galley, the rowers used long, heavy wooden oars to drive the ship forward, their pace set by the steady beating of a drum.

Galleys also had sails to catch the wind. The best feature of galleys was that they could move forward with or without wind, using sails, rowers, or both. This was an advantage in the Mediterranean Sea, where the winds often die out. When the wind failed, a galley was not stranded. The captain simply ordered the rowers to work. During sea battles, the rowers had to follow orders with speed and strength in order to get the galleys into position to either fire their cannon at the enemy or to ram the enemy's ships.

Most of the men who rowed galleys were slaves who had been captured in war or thrown into prison for debt or for their crimes. A galley slave who had been captured might be ransomed, that is, bought out of slavery, if his family, friends, or government could afford to buy his freedom.

Many of the ships belonging to Barbarossa and some other Turkish captains, however, were **galleots**, smaller versions of galleys. Their smaller size meant that they were armed with fewer, smaller cannons than the galleys could carry. On the other hand, galleots were nimble, speedy, and easy to maneuver. Galleots needed fewer rowers than galleys did. Aboard their galleots, Turkish captains often used free soldiers, sailors, or personal followers, rather than slaves, to man the oars. This meant that the rowers were also fighting men. It also meant that the Turkish captains did not have to fear the threat of a slave **mutiny** during battle.

A third type of ship had begun to appear in the Mediterranean by Barbarossa's day. This was the **galleon**, larger than the galley and powered only by sails, with no rowers. Galleons were similar to the ships that the European nations were using to explore the Atlantic and colonize the Americas. Their disadvantage in battle was that they needed

A Galley Slave's Life

Rowing a galley in Barbarossa's time was backbreaking, miserable work—and it was worse for slaves than for free men. J.M. Bergerac, a Frenchman who served as a galley slave in the eighteenth century, described the rower's life as it was two hundred years after Barbarossa:

The officer who is master of the galley slaves remains . . . with the captain to receive his orders. There are two under officers . . . armed with whips, with which they flog the totally naked bodies of the slaves. When the captain gives the order to row, the officer gives the signal with a silver whistle, which hangs on a cord around his neck. The signal is repeated by the under officers and very soon all the fifty oars strike the water as if one. Imagine six men chained to a bench as naked as the day they were born, one foot on the stretcher, the other raised and placed on the bench in front of them, holding in their hands an oar of immense weight, stretching their bodies . . . with arms extended to push the loom of the oar clear of the backs of those in front of them . . . . They plunge the blades of the oars into the water and throw themselves back, falling onto the seat, which bends beneath their weight. Sometimes the galley slaves row like this ten, twelve, even twenty hours at a stretch, without the slightest repose or rest. On these occasions the officers will go round, putting into the mouths of the wretched rowers pieces of bread soaked in wine to prevent them from fainting.

wind and were helpless without it. Their advantage was that they could carry more cannons, and larger ones, than galleys.

The Dawn of Battle

It was Barbarossa who chose the setting for what came to be called the Battle of Preveza. He knew that the European fleet was meeting in the Ionian Sea, between Greece and the "boot heel" of Italy. His fleet reached the area from the south before the European fleet was fully assembled. He ordered his ships to pass through a narrow channel and into a body of water known as the Gulf of Ambracia or the Gulf of Arta. Preveza stands on one of the two **spits** of land at the entrance to the channel.

By entering the gulf, Barbarossa gave his fleet a major advantage but also took a major risk. The advantage was that the European fleet could not attack the Turkish fleet. Ships could pass through the channel only a few at a time, not in a large mass. If the European vessels tried to enter the gulf, Barbarossa's fleet could pick them off one by one. In addition, the channel was too shallow for the largest galleons of the European fleet.

The risk was that if the European fleet blocked the entrance of the channel, Barbarossa had no escape. He and his fleet would be trapped inside the gulf. On the other hand, if the European fleet stayed close to the entrance of the channel, it faced disaster if one of the fearsome September storms of the area blew up. Bad weather could drive the European ships onto the rocky shore, while the Turkish ships would be sheltered in the calmer waters of the gulf.

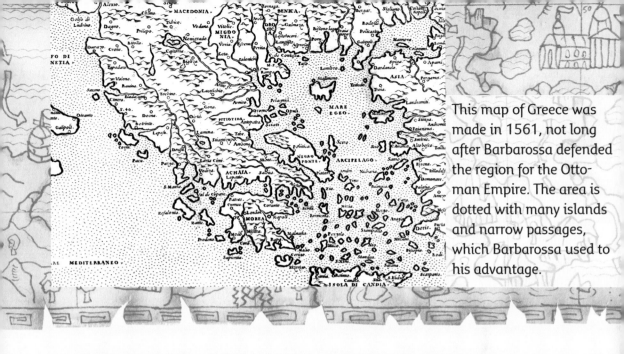

This map of Greece was made in 1561, not long after Barbarossa defended the region for the Ottoman Empire. The area is dotted with many islands and narrow passages, which Barbarossa used to his advantage.

Military historians think that Barbarossa, who knew the weather and seas of the Mediterranean as well as anyone, made a smart decision when he entered the Gulf of Ambracia. However, with one fleet inside the gulf and the other outside it, and neither commander willing to send his ships through the dangerous channel, how would the two forces ever meet in battle?

On the morning of September 27 the Turkish lookouts on the hills near Preveza woke to an unexpected sight. The European ships were moving away, heading south down the Ionian Sea, into Ottoman territory. Clearly their commander expected Barbarossa to follow in order to protect the sultan's lands. Leaving the Gulf of Ambracia, however, would mean that Barbarossa would be giving up his advantage.

Barbarossa did not hesitate. He gave the order for the Turkish fleet to raise its anchors and set out through the channel and into the open sea, chasing down the ships of the Europeans.

two

The Barbarossa Brothers

Kheir-ed-Din Barbarossa, the pirate who became an honored military commander, was given the name Khizr by his parents. For the first part of his career he was overshadowed by his brother Aruj. Together the two men became the most feared pirates of the Mediterranean Sea.

Island Beginnings

The birthplace of the Barbarossas was Mytilene, the capital city of the island of Lesbos in the Aegean Sea between Greece and Turkey. Lesbos had been a **colony** of ancient Greece. Later it passed to the

The Barbarossa brothers grew up on an island and became skilled sailors on the waters of the eastern Mediterranean Sea.

Byzantine Empire. The Ottomans took over Lesbos in 1462. Not long after, sometime in the 1470s, the Barbarossas were born.

The Barbarossas were most likely not Turkish by birth. Their father had served in the Turkish army, but he is said to have been a **janissary**, a soldier who was kidnapped as a young child from Christian parents and raised to be a faithful Muslim and an Ottoman warrior. He retired from service on Lesbos, started a pottery business, and married a local woman of Greek ancestry. They had four sons and two daughters. The sons were Aruj, Elias, Isaac, and Khizr.

Like most islanders, the boys became familiar with boats and sailing as they grew up. Aruj may have started his career by working on the boat that carried his father's pottery wares to market. Legends say that by the time Aruj became captain of his own galleot, Khizr was working for him as a rower. Aruj, Isaac, and Khizr all became seamen and traders, piloting small galleots from port to port around the Mediterranean.

Historians do not know for sure, but the brothers probably became corsairs at this time, too. Because the Ottomans and the European Christians were competing for control of the Mediterranean, captains on each side mixed business with piracy. It was normal to take advantage of any chance to attack the other side's ships, islands, or coastal towns.

The Knights of St. John

One of the fiercest enemies the Ottomans faced in the Mediterranean was the Order of the Knights of St. John. The order was a group of

Bodrum Castle, on Turkey's southwestern coast, was built by the Order of the Knights of St. John. These Christian warriors maintained several strongholds in Turkish territory.

Christian warriors dedicated to combating Islam as well as Arab and Turkish ships. Their headquarters was the Aegean island of Rhodes, but they also held fortresses on the coast of Turkey and elsewhere.

On one of Aruj's voyages he had the bad luck to cross paths with a large, well-armed galley belonging to the Knights. The Knights fired cannons at Aruj's galleot, disabling it. Some accounts say that either Elias or Isaac had sailed with his brother and was killed in this attack. Aruj and his surviving crew were taken prisoner.

A Man of Many Names

Kheir-ed-Din Barbarossa was known by more than one name during his lifetime. In the centuries since then, his Turkish and Arabic names and titles have been spelled a number of different ways in English.

The man who would later become the admiral of the Ottoman sultan's fleet was given the name Khizr (or Hizir) by his parents. There is no record of the family having a second name. So where did "Barbarossa" come from?

The Turkish version of the story says that after Spain outlawed the Muslim religion in 1502, Aruj used his ships to carry Muslim refugees from Spain to North Africa. The grateful refugees called him Baba Aruj, which means "Father Aruj." To Europeans this sounded like "Barbarossa," which means "Redbeard" in Italian, and Aruj did have a red beard. (Europeans of the twelfth century had given the same nickname to Frederick I, head of the **Holy Roman Empire**, because of his red beard.) European sources from the time simply say that Aruj was called Barbarossa because of his beard.

Images of Barbarossa always showed his reddish beard. Here he wears finery and brandishes weapons.

The "Barbarossa" or "Redbeard" nickname spread to include Khizr, whose beard was reddish-brown. Later in Khizr's career the sultan gave him the honorary name Kheir-ed-Din, which means "goodness of Islam," and the title *pasha*, which is similar to "lord" or "governor." Although Barbarossa went down in Turkish history as Barbaros Kheir-ed-Din Pasha, English sources usually give his name as Kheir-ed-Din (or Hayreddin) Barbarossa.

Like most prisoners of war, Aruj found himself chained to a bench, rowing one of the enemy's galleys. He served for at least a year. There are different accounts of what happened next, but the most believable version says that he and other Muslim galley slaves were ransomed and regained their freedom. It is not known who paid Aruj's ransom. Whether it was his family, the merchants who had helped pay for his galleot, or one of the Arab or Ottoman rulers is unknown. Khizr, however, seems to have delivered the ransom.

Soon afterward, the brothers somehow got hold of two galleots, powered by about seventeen oars on each side. The galleots were crewed by Turks who had chosen to join the brothers in return for a share of the profits. Trade and business were behind Aruj and Khizr now. They set themselves up as pirates.

The Barbary Coast

The brothers Aruj and Khizr shifted to full-time piracy around the year 1500. Soon afterward, they also switched the location of their activities away from the eastern end of the Mediterranean Sea. They moved west to the region known as the **Barbary Coast**.

The Barbary Coast was the name given to the Mediterranean coast of North Africa between Egypt and the Strait of Gibraltar, which is the passage from the Mediterranean into the Atlantic Ocean. Although North Africa contains an abundance of mountains and deserts, stretches of the coastline are green and fertile. Cities have flourished there since

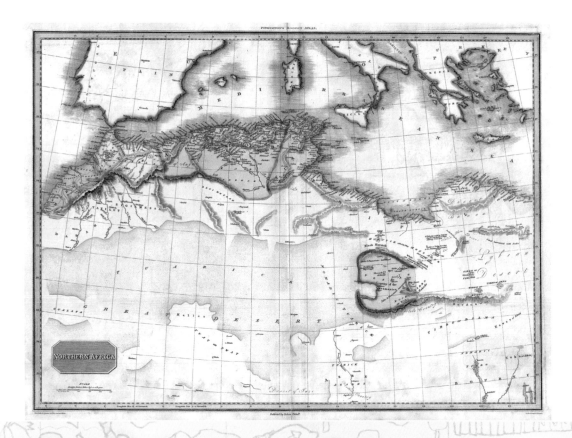

Made in 1818 in Scotland, this map highlights the Arab kingdoms of North Africa. These Muslim realms and Christian Europe often waged war on one another.

ancient times. The people of the region were known as Berbers, and the term "Barbary" comes from their name. They were Muslims but did not officially belong to the Ottoman Empire. In time Aruj and Khizr would give the Ottomans a foothold on the Barbary Coast.

The brothers' first base of operations along the coast was just outside the city of Tunis in what is now the nation of Tunisia. The local sultan welcomed them because they agreed to turn over a portion of their

The galleys of Ottoman and European navies clash in this battle scene. Billows of smoke everywhere show the importance of ships' cannons.

booty and captives to him. In 1504, Aruj brought a magnificent **prize** back to the port of Tunis. He had captured two large galleys belonging to Pope Julius II.

Aruj had taken the first galley off the coast of Italy by surprising its crew, sweeping his galleot alongside so that his men could leap aboard the papal galley and overwhelm its captain and officers. He quickly forced the European officers to take off their clothes, which he and his own men put on. When the second galley came into view, its captain saw men on the deck of the first galley, wearing familiar European clothing. He did not know that the galley had been taken by pirates. By the time he realized his mistake, he was too close to escape. Aruj and his men fired on the second galley, ran the first one alongside it, and swarmed onto its deck.

Aruj now controlled two fine galleys. He freed the Muslim galley slaves but left the Christian criminals and debtors in their chains. With his own free men and the remaining slaves at the oars, Aruj's two new ships made their way to Tunis, towing his galleot. He had captured many prisoners who would bring high ransoms, as well as money, goods, and new Christian slaves.

Soon after, the brothers used their galleys to capture a large Spanish galleon that could not escape from them because the wind upon which it depended had died. As word spread of the brothers' exploits, men came to join them, and they acquired more ships and crews. They continued to use free fighting men at the oars, rather than slaves. This advantage made up for the fact that their ships were smaller than most of the Christians' vessels. By this time the brothers had acquired the nickname "Barbarossa." From then on that is how they were known across the Mediterranean.

three

From Corsair to Admiral

The Barbarossa brothers became the sea wolves of the western Mediterranean. They preyed on the merchant ships of Spain, France, and the two rich and powerful Italian city-states of Genoa and Venice. They also attacked the Christians' coastal towns and fortresses, including Naples and Sicily, which are now part of Italy but were controlled by Spain at that time. Although Aruj would eventually fall in battle, Khizr's fortunes rose.

Leaping up from their smaller galleot, Aruj and his men attack a galley belonging to the Catholic Church. This victorious attack laid the foundation for the Barbarossas' fortunes.

Westward to Algiers

By 1510, relations between the Barbarossa brothers and the sultan of Tunis had grown tense. The corsairs were tired of turning over part of their booty to the sultan. They decided to move south to the island of Djerba, which the sultan let them occupy for free in return for defending it from the Spanish.

Two years later, however, the Barbarossas received an invitation from the sultan of Bougie, an Arab city on the Barbary Coast west of Tunis. The Spanish had conquered Bougie and driven the sultan into hiding in the mountains. He wanted the corsairs to help him get his city back. With their fleet of twelve ships, the Barbarossas and their followers set out for Bougie. When they arrived, they ordered the cannons from their galleots to be carried ashore. Then they began bombarding the wall that surrounded the city.

The cannon fire eventually created a break in the wall. Aruj then rushed through to the head of a troop of fighters. A shot from a Spanish gun tore off his left arm and he fell to the ground. Shocked, his men retreated, carrying their leader. Aruj survived and eventually replaced his left arm with one made of silver. In the meantime, the Barbarossas set up a new base of operations in a sheltered harbor near Algiers, in what is now the nation of Algeria.

In 1516, Aruj killed the sultan of Algiers and took over the city. The following year Algiers became part of the Ottoman Empire.

The Ottoman sultan made Aruj its pasha, the title given to the local ruler of the sultan's territories. In spite of their new position as lords, the Barbarossas continued to operate their corsair fleet.

Aruj did not rule Algiers for long. In 1517 he was killed in battle against Spanish forces that were trying to capture a North African town. Khizr became the new pasha of Algiers, and the sultan gave him a new name: Kheir-ed-Din. He was already known to be a skilled captain and a fearsome corsair. He would soon outshine his older brother's achievements.

A portrait that is believed to be Andrea Doria, Barbarossa's rival, in his old age.

Barbarossa's Greatest Rival

For decades Kheir-ed-Din Barbarossa had one great rival among the seamen of the Mediterranean: Andrea Doria. The son of a noble family in Genoa, Doria trained as a soldier and sailor, then rose to become Genoa's leading naval commander.

Doria had first clashed with the Barbarossas in 1512, when he and his men had captured some galleots from the Barbarossas' base near Tunis. He almost clashed with Kheir-ed-Din Barbarossa in 1519. At that time,

A storm drives ships onto rocks along the Barbary Coast of North Africa. Whole fleets were wrecked in this way.

the king of Spain had gathered a fleet of ships from many European countries to drive the Turks out of North Africa. Doria commanded the fourteen galleys that Genoa contributed to the fleet.

The European fleet got a late start. It was caught in an early autumn storm and driven onto the North African coast. Many ships were wrecked, some were seized by the waiting Turks, and the rest retreated. Ernle Bradford, a naval historian who wrote about the life of Barbarossa in his book *The Sultan's Admiral*, calls this "one of the worst disasters in the storm-clouded history of the North African coast." Doria escaped, however. He and Barbarossa would meet again in the future.

Throughout the 1520s, Barbarossa ruled Algiers for the Ottoman sultan and continued to attack the ships and settlements of Christian nations around the western Mediterranean. He repeatedly raided the Balearic Islands, off the coast of Spain. He also attacked the islands of Sardinia, Sicily, and Corsica, off the Italian coast. He continued Aruj's practice of ferrying thousands of Muslim refugees from Spain to North Africa.

In 1531, Andrea Doria led a fleet of twenty Spanish galleys in an attack on the coast of Algeria. Barbarossa drove off the attackers, but Doria soon stepped up his activities in the central Mediterranean. He raided Ottoman villages and towns in the Ionian Sea, easily defeating the Turkish navy in its home waters. Suleiman, the Ottoman sultan, realized that he needed to do something to make his navy more effective. In 1533, he sent a messenger to Algiers to ask the famous corsair Barbarossa to come to Constantinople.

The Pirate Admiral

Kheir-ed-Din Barbarossa, who had been born a humble soldier's son and was known to all as a pirate, left Algiers in high honor, summoned by the sultan. Little is known of Barbarossa's private or family life, but he had a son, Hassan, whose mother was Algerian. Barbarossa placed Hassan in charge of Algiers when he left. Barbarossa was never to return to Algiers.

On his way to Constantinople, Barbarossa kept up his corsair ways. He captured several galleys loaded with grain that was being shipped from Sicily to Spain. When he arrived in the Ottoman capital

Castello di Barbarossa.

he presented gifts to the sultan: camels carrying gold and jewels, Christian slaves, and animals from Africa such as lions.

The nobles of Constantinople, and the high-ranking political and military leaders of the empire, had gathered to get their first look at the famous corsair. They would soon get used to the sight of him, for Constantinople became his home.

The sultan put Barbarossa in charge of overhauling the Ottoman navy, including building new ships, training officers, and merging his band of battle-hardened followers with the sultan's own troops. Barbarossa was made admiral of the Ottoman fleet. His task was to prepare the Turkish navy to meet and defeat the navies of Christian Europe and their chief commander, Andrea Doria.

In his first big campaign with the Turkish navy, Barbarossa raided the coast of Italy in 1534. He then turned south to capture Tunis from its Arab sultan. This upset Charles V, king of Spain and Holy Roman Emperor, who feared that a Turkish stronghold in Tunis would be more troublesome to his territories in Sicily and Italy than the old sultan had been. In 1535, Charles pulled together a fleet, including Doria and his ships, to attack Tunis.

The European attack on Tunis succeeded, in part because Christian slaves inside the city rebelled and joined the attackers. Barbarossa abandoned Tunis but took his revenge on the emperor by attacking a series of towns and cities in Italy and Spain. The next year he led two hundred Ottoman ships in a series of attacks on Charles's possessions in Italy. In 1537 he seized a number of islands that had belonged to the sea-going Republic of Venice in Italy.

By this time the pope had had enough of Barbarossa's attacks on Christian nations and people. In 1538, he called on all of Europe to form a great fleet that would crush the Ottoman navy once and for all. That fleet was put under the command of Andrea Doria, who ordered it to sail to Preveza to meet Barbarossa's Ottoman navy. After the standoff between the commanders, with Barbarossa inside the Gulf of Ambracia and Doria blocking the channel, it was Doria who ordered the European

Under Barbarossa's leadership, the Ottoman navy crushed the European fleet at the Battle of Preveza despite being outnumbered and outgunned.

ships to sail southward. He had hoped to draw Barbarossa out of the gulf and into a position where he could be attacked.

The Battle of Preveza

Doria had a difficult job commanding the European fleet because it contained two kinds of ships: galleys with oars and galleons without oars. When winds were good, the galleons swept ahead and the galleys had hard work to keep pace with them. When the wind fell, the galleons stood idle. As a result Doria's fleet became strung out in a long line between the Greek coast and the island of Levkas, or Lefkada.

Doria's plan was to head south toward a Turkish settlement. Barbarossa would have to defend the Turkish settlement, which would force him to fight. Doria, with 157 ships, believed he would have an advantage over Barbarossa's 122 smaller ships. To Doria's surprise, the Turkish fleet caught up with him sooner than he had expected, and before he had arranged his fleet for battle.

The largest ship of Doria's fleet, a huge battle galleon with large cannons, was stranded without wind and lagged far behind the rest of the European ships. The Turkish fleet attacked it repeatedly. The big ship's cannons destroyed or disabled several Ottoman galleys, but the Turks kept coming at it, and Doria did not come to its rescue. The battle galleon survived and finally escaped, but Doria had wasted much time maneuvering his fleet to try to trap the Ottoman vessels.

In the end Doria failed to get into a position from which he wanted to fight. The nimble galleys and galleots of the Turks picked off the stragglers among Doria's ships. They managed to capture more than half a dozen. Some historians have suggested that Doria did not want to risk the ships that were his own property. Whatever the reason, once Doria saw that the battle was not going to be easily won, he retreated. This left the Turks victorious.

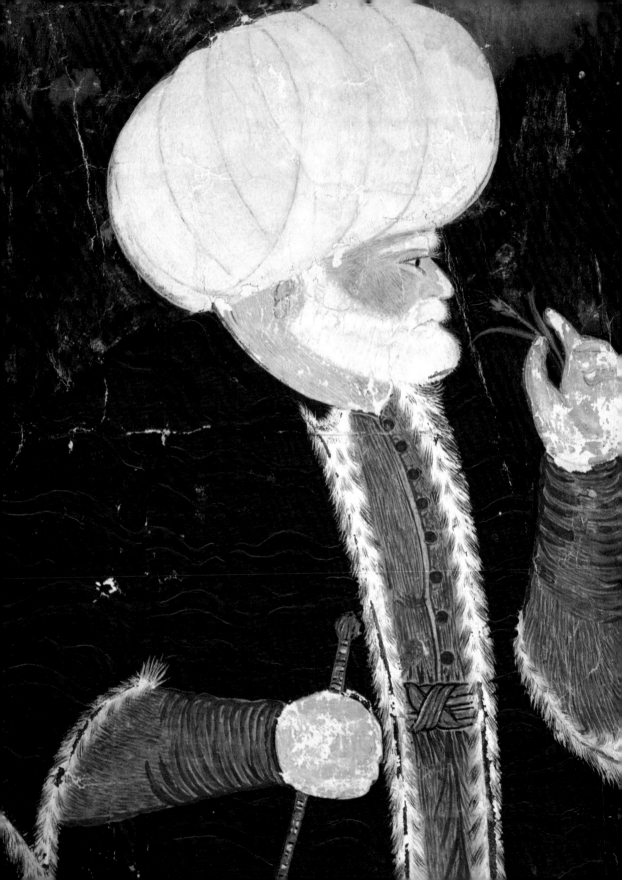

Last Years
and Legacy

The Battle of Preveza proved that the Turkish navy had become a major force in the Mediterranean. During the following year Barbarossa captured most of the remaining Venetian or Spanish lands in the central and western Mediterranean. A 1540 treaty with Venice gave the Ottoman Empire control of most of the Mediterranean, and much of the credit belongs to the pirate-turned-admiral Barbarossa.

This portrait of Barbarossa toward the end of his life, painted between 1540 and 1545, is part of the collection of the Topkapi Museum in Istanbul.

Charles V, the Holy Roman Emperor, tried to get Barbarossa to switch sides and work for him—but failed.

Last Adventures

Also in 1540, Holy Roman Emperor Charles V sent a message to Barbarossa, offering him a rich reward if he would change sides and become the high admiral of Charles's fleet. Barbarossa said no. Three years later he led a fleet of 210 ships into the western Mediterranean. By this time France had become an ally of the Ottoman Empire, and Barbarossa joined French forces in a series of attacks on Spanish and Italian territories. He was ready to sail up Italy's Tiber River to attack Rome, but the king of France asked him not to attack the pope's city.

Barbarossa had lost neither his naval skill nor his passion for combat. In 1544, he once again defeated a Spanish and Italian fleet. He also took his fleet to Genoa to demand the release of Turgut Reis, an Ottoman officer who had been imprisoned there since 1540. Legend says that Barbarossa met with Andrea Doria at Doria's own home to agree upon a ransom for Turgut. Barbarossa's final voyage was in 1545, when he fired cannons at the coast of Spain and landed to raid Spain's Balearic Islands for the last time.

Unlike many pirates, Kheir-ed-Din Barbarossa had a quiet death. He had built a palace on the outskirts of Constantinople. It sat on the shore of the Bosphorus, a waterway that separates Europe and Asia, so that his ships could anchor nearby. There Barbarossa died of a fever in 1546, a year after he retired from the sea. His mausoleum, or aboveground tomb, is now surrounded by Barbaros Park in Istanbul. A statue in his honor stands in the park, which was named after him.

Barbarossa's Legacy

Barbarossa spread terror and calamity in the Spanish and Italian lands that border the Mediterranean Sea. His name was remembered in those lands for a long time. Many old stone towers on the coasts and islands of Italy and Spain are still called "Barbarossa towers" because it is said that people used to watch from them for the dreaded sight of Turkish ships approaching.

Beyond his piratical adventures, Barbarossa had a huge impact on history. He helped bring North Africa under the control of the Ottoman Empire. Above all, he made the Turks rulers of the Mediterranean in the mid-sixteenth century.

Ottoman power in the Mediterranean would not be shaken until 1571. That year another massive European fleet, gathered by another pope, defeated the Ottoman navy in the Battle of Lepanto, not far from Preveza.

The Dashing Corsair

Even Barbarossa's enemies admitted that he was brave and bold. Europeans hated and feared the Muslim corsairs, but sometimes they also admired their daring. As time went on, favorable images of corsairs began to appear in European literature and art. These corsairs were seen as romantic, dashing individuals who loved freedom and rebelled against the rules and limits of society. Whether they were Christian or Muslim, the corsairs in this romantic vision were portrayed as colorful, exotic, and heroic figures, although they often were tragic figures as well.

This romantic view of the corsair got a big boost from the English poet George Gordon, Lord Byron. In 1813, he published a poem titled *The Bride of Abydos*. It is set in Turkey and features the doomed love between a pirate and the sultan's daughter. A year later he published a long poem titled *The Corsair*, which became a best seller. Its hero is a moody young man who is at war with society but is irresistibly attractive to women. (This was Byron's image of himself.) The Corsair was later turned into an opera by the Italian composer Giuseppe Verdi. It also inspired a ballet.

Nineteenth-century Spanish artist Juan Luna created this vision of the Battle of Lepanto. The Ottomans were defeated by Europeans twenty-five years after Redbeard's death.

By that time, Barbarossa was becoming a legend. More than five centuries after his death, his name lives on in the names of streets, restaurants, and other landmarks in Istanbul and throughout Turkey. He is considered a national hero, sometimes called "King of the Sea."

The long conflict between Christian Europe and Muslim Turkey shaped the course of Barbarossa's life. To Europeans, Barbarossa was a corsair, and he did commit many acts of piracy in his long career. To the Ottomans, on the other hand, he was a heroic defender of their faith. The career of Kheir-ed-Din Barbarossa is a reminder that the same person may be seen as a villain or as a hero, depending upon who is looking.

Timeline

1299   Muslim peoples of central and eastern Turkey
unite under Osman I and begin building an empire;
they are later known in Europe as the Ottomans.

1453   The Ottomans conquer the Christian city of
Constantinople (later called Istanbul) and make it the
capital of the Ottoman Empire.

1470s   The brothers Aruj and Khizr, later known as the
Barbarossas, are born in the town of Mytilene on
the island of Lesbos.

ca. 1500   Aruj and Khizr become full-time corsairs.

ca. 1504   The Barbarossa brothers set up headquarters near
the port of Tunis.

1504   Aruj captures two galleys belonging to Pope Julius II.

1510   The Barbarossas move to the island of Djerba,
south of Tunis.

1512   Aruj is defeated in battle against the Spanish at Bougie
and loses an arm.

1516	Aruj conquers and takes control of Algiers.
1517	Algiers becomes part of the Ottoman Empire.
1518	Aruj is killed in battle against the Spanish; Khizr, now called Kheir-ed-Din Barbarossa, takes his place as ruler of Algiers.
1531	Kheir-ed-Din Barbarossa defeats the Genoese admiral Andrea Doria in a sea battle.
1532	Barbarossa defeats Doria again, sails to Istanbul, and meets the Ottoman sultan, who names him Grand Admiral of the Ottoman navy and chief ruler of North Africa.
1538	Barbarossa defeats the Christian fleet of the Holy Roman Empire, commanded by Doria, at Preveza, giving the Ottomans control of the Mediterranean Sea.
1545	Barbarossa retires to his palace in Istanbul.
1546	Barbarossa dies in Istanbul.

Glossary

admiral A top-ranking naval commander.

Barbary Coast The Mediterranean coast of North Africa, between Egypt and the Atlantic Ocean.

booty The money, goods, or other loot obtained by piracy.

colony A territory outside a country's borders that is claimed, controlled, or settled by that country.

corsair A term for pirates who operated in the Mediterranean Sea.

emir Chieftain or leader of a group or tribe among the Islamic peoples.

galleon A large sailing ship used by Europeans in the sixteenth century.

galleot A small, nimble version of a galley, favored by the Turkish corsairs.

galley A type of ship that has both sails and oars, good for use in conditions of little or no wind.

Holy Roman Empire A collection of states and city-states in Europe that lasted from 800 to 1806 and was supposed to be a Christian continuation of the ancient Roman empire.

janissary A soldier of the Ottoman Empire who was taken from his parents (who were often Christians in conquered territories) and raised as a Muslim warrior.

mutiny An act of rebellion by sailors or crewmen against their captain or other officers.

Ottoman Empire A Muslim kingdom that originated in central Turkey in 1299 and grew to cover the Middle East, North Africa, Greece and part of Eastern Europe, and many Mediterranean islands.

pasha A Turkish title similar to "lord" or "governor."

prize A ship captured at sea.

reis A Turkish title meaning "captain."

spit A small point of land commonly consisting of sand or gravel deposited by waves and currents and running into a body of water.

sultan Supreme ruler.

Find Out More

Books

Gilkerson, William. *A Thousand Years of Pirates*. Plattsburgh, NY: Tundra Books, 2010.

Krull, Kathleen. *Lives of the Pirates*. New York, NY: HMH Books for Young Readers, 2010.

Malam, John. *The Barbarossa Brothers and the Pirates of the Mediterranean*. Dover, DE: QEB Publishing, 2008.

Websites

Barbarossa

ww.allaboutturkey.com/barbaros.htm

The All About Turkey website has a short biography of Barbarossa.

A Brief History of Piracy

www.royalnavalmuseum.org/info_sheets_piracy.htm

The Royal Naval Museum of Great Britain explains what piracy is, with a short overview of the history of pirates. The Ottoman corsairs are mentioned.

Ottoman Sailing Ships

www.turkishculture.org/military/naval/ottoman-ships-758.htm?type=1

This page, part of the Turkish Cultural Foundation's website, describes the history of the Ottoman navy and how it helped build the Ottoman Empire. It also includes a brief mention of Barbarossa.

Museums

The New England Pirate Museum

www.piratemuseum.com/pirate.html

Located in Salem, Massachusetts, this museum features a walking tour through the world of pirates, including recreations of a dockside village, ship, and a cave. Also on display are authentic pirate treasures.

The St. Augustine Pirate and Treasure Museum

www.thepiratemuseum.com

This interactive museum covers 300 years of pirate history, and boasts many artifacts including pirate loot, a real treasure chest, and one of only three surviving Jolly Roger flags.

Bibliography

Bradford, Ernle. *The Sultan's Admiral: Barbarossa—Pirate and Empire Builder*. New York, NY: Tauris Parke, 2009. Originally published 1968.

Cordingly, David. *Under the Black Flag: The Romance and Reality of Life among the Pirates*. New York, NY: Random House, 2013.

Konstam, Angus, with Roger Michael Kean. *Pirates: Predators of the Seas*. New York, NY: Skyhorse Publishing, 2007.

Rogozinski, Jan. *Pirates!* New York, NY: Facts On File, 1995.

Travers, Tim. *Pirates: A History*. Stroud, UK: Tempus Publishing, 2007.

Wolf, John. *The Barbary Coast: Algiers Under the Turks, 1500–1830*. New York, NY: Norton, 1979.

Index

About the Author

Rebecca Stefoff has written books for young readers on many topics in history, science, exploration, and literature. She is the author of the six-volume series Is It Science? (Cavendish Square, 2014) and the four-volume series Animal Behavior Revealed (Cavendish Square, 2014). Although she has scuba-dived in sunken shipwrecks in the Atlantic Ocean and the Caribbean Sea, she has yet to see her first pirate ship. You can learn more about Stefoff and her books for young people at rebeccastefoff.com.